ANCIENT ROME

ANCIENT

BLASTOFF!
DISCOVERY

BY EMILY ROSE OACHS

BELLWETHER MEDIA   MINNEAPOLIS, MN

Blastoff! Discovery launches a new mission: reading to learn. Filled with facts and features, each book offers you an exciting new world to explore!

This edition first published in 2020 by Bellwether Media, Inc.

No part of this publication may be reproduced in whole or in part without written permission of the publisher.
For information regarding permission, write to Bellwether Media, Inc.,
Attention: Permissions Department,
6012 Blue Circle Drive, Minnetonka, MN 55343.

Library of Congress Cataloging-in-Publication Data

Names: Oachs, Emily Rose, author.
Title: Ancient Rome / By Emily Rose Oachs.
Description: Minneapolis, MN : Bellwether Media, Inc., [2020] |
   Series: Blastoff! Discovery: Ancient civilizations | Includes bibliographical
   references and index. | Audience: Ages 7-13 | Audience: Grades 4-6 |
   Summary: "Engaging images accompany information about ancient
   Rome. The combination of high-interest subject matter and narrative text
   is intended for students in grades 3 through 8"– Provided by publisher.
Identifiers: LCCN 2019036006 (print) | LCCN 2019036007 (ebook) |
   ISBN 9781644871805 (library binding) | ISBN 9781618918642
   (paperback) | ISBN 9781618918567 (ebook)
Subjects: LCSH: Rome–Civilization–Juvenile literature. | Rome–History
   Juvenile literature. | Rome–Social life and customs–Juvenile literature.
Classification: LCC DG77 .O23 2020 (print) | LCC DG77 (ebook) |
   DDC 937–dc23
LC record available at https://lccn.loc.gov/2019036006
LC ebook record available at https://lccn.loc.gov/2019036007

Editor: Kate Moening   Designer: Jeffrey Kollock

Printed in the United States of America, North Mankato, MN.

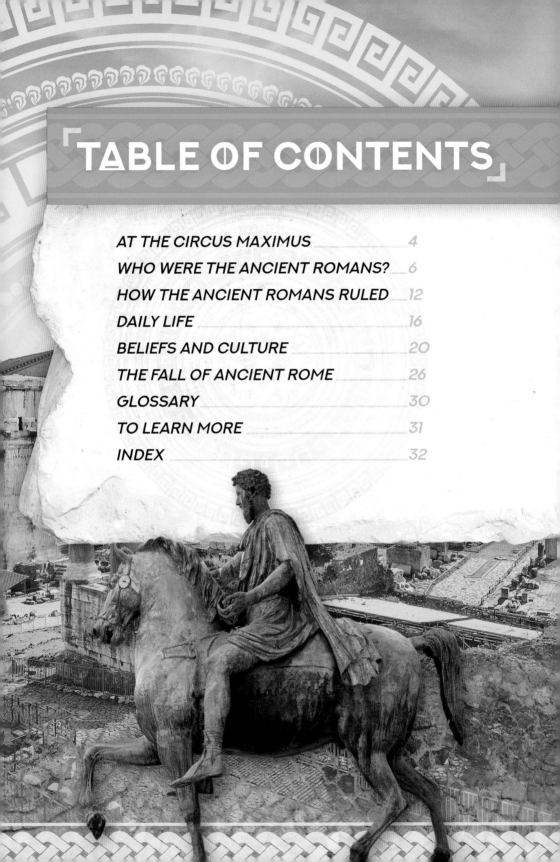

TABLE OF CONTENTS

AT THE CIRCUS MAXIMUS

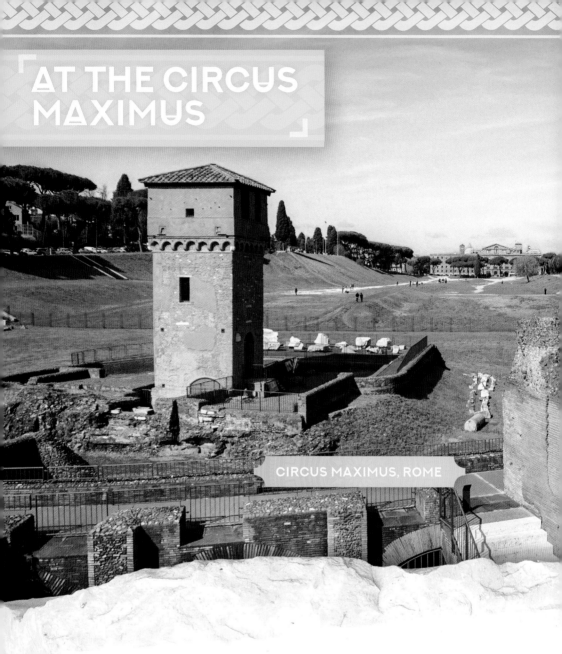

CIRCUS MAXIMUS, ROME

A boy and his father approach the Circus Maximus **arena**. The huge building stands in the center of Rome. Thousands of excited Romans push through the rows of archways. The boy's father squeezes them into some open seats.

CHARIOT RACE

Soon, the race begins. Teams of horses burst from the starting gates. They sprint around the track pulling chariots. The boy claps and cheers loudly. He loves afternoons at the chariot races in the Roman Empire!

WHO WERE THE ANCIENT ROMANS?

ROMAN FORUM, ROME

Ancient Rome began in what is now Italy. The civilization lasted from 753 BCE until 476 CE. Over centuries, it became a broad empire.

The Roman Empire reached its largest size around 117 CE. A powerful military helped it spread across three continents. At its height, Rome's rule reached today's Britain, Egypt, and Iraq. The empire numbered about 60 million people. About one in four people alive on Earth lived under Roman rule!

117 CE ROMAN EMPIRE

N
W · E
S

KEY — Roman Empire

BLACK SEA

MEDITERRANEAN SEA

Rome's location made it easy to exchange goods and ideas with many different cultures. Rome was founded along the Tiber River. The river created a clear trade route to the Mediterranean Sea. Wealth from trade helped Rome grow.

Rome gained strength by embracing other cultures. Romans learned about trade from the Etruscans to the north. Much of Roman religion came from the Greeks to the east. Bringing in other cultures built loyalty to Rome as areas were taken over.

OVERLOOK OF TIBER RIVER

CASTEL SANT'ANGELO
AND TIBER RIVER, ROME

THE FOUNDING MYTH

Stories claimed that twin brothers founded Rome. Romulus and Remus were raised by a wolf. They built Rome near where the wolf first found them. The city was named after Romulus.

Ancient Rome is remembered for its feats of engineering. From 312 BCE, **aqueducts** brought water to Roman cities. One of the longest stretched 60 miles (97 kilometers) long! These structures allowed for running water, fountains, and Rome's famous public baths.

PONT DU GARD AQUEDUCT

THINK ABOUT IT

Aqueducts allowed Romans to build cities in places without nearby water. How could this freedom make Rome more powerful?

⌜CONCRETE⌟

Rome was the first civilization to use concrete widely. A special mineral strengthened the mixture of limestone, volcanic ash, and seawater. Concrete buildings were strong and lasting. This supported the growth of the civilization.

HOW CONCRETE HELPED THE ROMAN CIVILIZATION GROW

- ✅ aqueducts allowed people to settle in places without a nearby water supply
- ✅ sea walls protected cities and trade ships
- ✅ sewers drained baths, toilets, and storm water out of cities
- ✅ arched bridges helped roads cross water to connect the empire
- ✅ new designs such as domes, arches, and vaults could be built

Romans also built a vast network of roads. By 200 CE, more than 50,000 miles (80,467 kilometers) of road connected the empire. Soldiers, goods, and ideas could reach Rome's faraway territories.

HOW THE ANCIENT ROMANS RULED

ROMAN SENATE

THINK ABOUT IT

How is the Roman Republic like the United States government today? How is it different?

Over the centuries, Rome had three different types of government. In each, a powerful group called the Senate advised Rome's leaders.

Monarchs called kings ruled after Rome's founding. In 509 BCE, Romans overthrew the monarchy to form a republic. Two leaders, called consuls, were elected yearly. The Roman Republic enjoyed centuries of wealth and growth. Julius Caesar brought about the Republic's fall. The Roman Empire rose in its place in 27 BCE. Emperors held total power over their subjects.

JULIUS CAESAR

WHO WAS JULIUS CAESAR?

general and politician in the Roman Republic

WHEN DID HE LIVE?

around 100 BCE to March 15, 44 BCE

WHERE DID HE LIVE?

city of Rome

WHAT WAS HE KNOWN FOR?

- elected consul in 59 BCE
- formed an alliance called the First Triumvirate
- conquered today's France and Belgium
- in 46 BCE, took public office as dictator
- in 44 BCE, declared himself dictator for life
- created the 365-day Julian calendar

WHY WAS HE IMPORTANT?

- led to the fall of the Republic of Rome
- his death led to civil wars and the Roman Empire
- First Triumvirate changed Roman government
- Julian calendar used widely for more than 1,500 years

ROME'S GOVERNMENTS

REGAL ROME
753 TO 509 BCE

GOVERNMENT

monarchy ruled by a king

KNOWN FOR

- six kings elected over time
- Roman mythology

ACHIEVEMENTS

- founding of the city of Rome
- written Latin language

ROMAN REPUBLIC
509 BCE TO 27 BCE

GOVERNMENT

- assemblies of citizens voted for leaders yearly
- elected leaders commanded army and proposed laws
- assemblies voted to pass laws

KNOWN FOR

- gladiator fights
- rule of Julius Caesar

ACHIEVEMENTS

- rapid expansion
- aqueducts

ROMAN EMPIRE
27 BCE TO 476 CE

GOVERNMENT

- complete power held by an emperor
- emperor viewed as a god and worshipped after death

KNOWN FOR

- popularity of grand public baths grows
- Christianity becomes the Empire's official religion

ACHIEVEMENTS

- peak empire size in 117 CE
- the Colosseum and Pantheon are built

FIRST PUNIC WAR

Rome's Latin founders lived alongside many other **ethnic** groups. Warfare brought many of these groups under Roman control. As Rome grew, it built a workforce of slaves from conquered lands.

Large trade networks also helped Rome gain wealth, power, and resources. Starting around 130 BCE, the **Silk Road** linked Roman lands to China. Traders brought valuable eastern goods, such as silk and spices. Water routes also moved items around the Mediterranean.

Roman social classes were decided by birth. Romans could not move from one class to another. During the Republic, wealthy **patricians** controlled Rome's government. Early on, **plebeians** could not hold office. But by 367 BCE, they could be elected as leaders.

At home, men had complete control over their families. They could choose children's spouses and even sell their children as slaves. Women took charge of life in the house. They cooked, spun thread, raised children, and handled the family's money.

Romans spent mornings working. Peasants were farmers, laborers, or shop owners. Wealthy Romans were often landowners. They earned money from the work of enslaved field workers. Some slaves were doctors or teachers.

Afternoons were a time to relax. Both wealthy and poor Romans visited grand public baths. These were places to exercise, bathe, and spend time with friends. Romans packed arenas such as the Colosseum for entertainment. They watched chariot races and deadly **gladiator** fights.

GLADIATOR FIGHT

COLOSSEUM, ROME

BELIEFS AND CULTURE

ROMAN RITUAL

Hundreds of spirits and gods were important in everyday life. Many were adopted from Rome's neighbors. Romans followed careful **rituals** to win the gods' favor. They made offerings and **sacrificed** animals. During the Empire, Romans also worshipped their emperors as gods to show thanks and support.

Toward the Republic's end, laws offered religious protection. This drew many Jews to Rome. In 313 CE, Emperor Constantine began allowing Christianity. Within 100 years, Christianity was the Empire's official religion.

ROMAN GODS

JUNO
- goddess of childbirth and marriage
- Greek origin

JUPITER
- god of sky
- Greek origin

MINERVA
- goddess of wisdom
- Etruscan origin

VENUS
- goddess of love and beauty
- Greek origin

MARS
- god of war
- Greek origin

JANUS
- god of beginnings and endings
- Roman origin

Most Romans spoke Latin. By 600 BCE, they had a written language. Romans wrote about myths, history, and philosophy. The first century BCE saw some of ancient Rome's greatest writers. These included the politician Cicero and poets Ovid and Virgil. Roman theater also drew from Greek writings. Writers copied the style of ancient Greek plays.

ANCIENT LATIN LETTERS

The 21 letters of the ancient Latin alphabet came from Etruscan writing. Later, two more letters were added from Greek writing. This made the classical Latin alphabet. It is the basis for many languages, including English! See if any of these Latin letters look familiar!

L	K	I	H	Z	F	E	D	C	B	A

X	U	T	S	R	Q	P	O	N	M

CICERO SPEAKING TO THE SENATE

Latin was also important for public speaking. During the Republic, skilled **orators** gave powerful speeches to the Senate. Speeches were meant to sway votes on issues.

THINK ABOUT IT

Roman emperors had large statues of themselves placed across the territory. What do you think they wanted to say to Roman citizens with these pieces?

ROMAN MOSAIC

Roman art varied widely. **Mosaics** of colored glass and pottery patterned floors and fountains. Metal coins featured gods, rulers, and battle scenes. Wall paintings showed people and nature.

Roman sculptures were usually cast in bronze or carved in marble. Early on, artists copied statues of the gods made by Greek sculptors. These works showed beautiful, perfect human figures. Over time, Roman artists created more natural sculptures. Giant statues of emperors also became common.

MARBLE BATTLE SCENE SCULPTURE

THE FALL OF ANCIENT ROME

ROMAN RUINS IN PALMYRA, SYRIA

No single problem caused Rome's fall. When the empire stopped growing, it had fewer new slaves. This slowed the economy. In 285 CE, the empire was split into two parts with co-emperors. After this happened, unstable leadership weakened the government.

Roman armies also struggled to defend against outside groups. In 476, a Germanic king overthrew Rome's western half. The Western Empire broke into small kingdoms ruled by outsiders. The Eastern Empire would continue for almost another 1,000 years. But ancient Roman civilization was over.

ROMAN TIMELINE

509 BCE
revolution leads to the creation of the Roman Republic

476 CE
Germanic king Odoacer unseats Roman emperor Romulus Augustulus

313 CE
Emperor Constantine allows the practice of Christianity

753 BCE
the city of Rome is founded

79 CE
Mount Vesuvius erupts, burying the city of Pompeii in a thick layer of volcanic ash

27 CE
civil wars end with the start of the Roman Empire and Augustus's reign

Today, ruins of buildings and roads still stand as reminders of Rome's strength. Sometimes, construction work accidentally unearths Roman ruins and **artifacts**.

UNEARTHING HISTORY

In 79 CE, Mount Vesuvius buried the city of Pompeii under thick ash. The ash perfectly preserved the city. Researchers even found jars of fruit and loaves of bread!

Roman culture also lives on. Many modern governments are based on the Roman Republic. Six of the eight planets were named after Roman gods. Spanish, Italian, and other **Romance languages** grew out of Latin. Almost 1,600 years after its fall, Rome's impact still reaches around the world!

MODERN ROME, ITALY

GLOSSARY

aqueducts—human-made channels that bring water from one place to another

arena—a large building where public entertainment takes place

artifacts—items made long ago by humans; artifacts tell people today about people from the past.

cultures—the specific beliefs and practices of groups or regions

ethnic—related to a group of people who share customs and an identity

Etruscans—an ancient civilization in central Italy that was most powerful between 700 and 300 BCE

gladiator—an ancient Roman fighter who would battle other gladiators for public entertainment

monarchs—people who rule over kingdoms

mosaics—decorations that use pieces of colored glass or tile to make pictures or patterns

orators—powerful public speakers

patricians—wealthy citizens of ancient Rome; patricians came from the original citizen families of Rome.

philosophy—the study of ideas about knowledge, thinking, and the meaning of life

plebeians—commoners in ancient Rome

republic—a type of government in which citizens vote for representatives to rule

rituals—religious ceremonies or practices

Romance languages—modern languages whose origins are in the Latin language; Spanish, Italian, French, Portuguese, and Romanian are all Romance languages.

sacrificed—made an offering of something valuable to the gods

Silk Road—a system of trade routes that connected the Mediterranean with ancient China, starting around 130 BCE

TO LEARN MORE

AT THE LIBRARY

Chrisp, Peter. *Rome.* New York, N.Y.: DK Publishing, 2016.

O'Connor, Jim. *Where Is the Colosseum?* New York, N.Y.: Grosset & Dunlap, 2017.

Stokes, Jonathan W. *The Thrifty Guide to Ancient Rome: A Handbook for Time Travelers.* New York, N.Y.: Viking, 2018.

ON THE WEB

FACTSURFER

Factsurfer.com gives you a safe, fun way to find more information.

1. Go to www.factsurfer.com.

2. Enter "ancient Rome" into the search box and click 🔍.

3. Select your book cover to see a list of related web sites.

INDEX

The images in this book are reproduced through the courtesy of: S.Borisov, cover; immfocus studio, p. 3; GoodLifeStudio, pp. 4-5; The Print Collector/ Alamy, p. 5; Yasonya, pp. 6-7; Viacheslav Lopatin, pp. 8, 14 (landscape), 28 (fun fact); cge2010, pp. 8-9, 10; Astridlike, p. 9 (fun fact); serato, p. 11 (concrete); Stefano_Valeri, p. 11 (left), 11 (middle); Leonid Andronov, p. 11 (right); Chronicle/ Alamy, p. 12; Gilmanshin, p. 13 (Caesar); Mazur Travel, p. 13 (Rome); North Wind Picture Archives/ Alamy, p. 15; Fab38, pp. 16-17; Chris Hellier/ Alamy, pp. 17 (top), 24-25; Lebrecht Music & Arts/ Alamy, p. 17 (right); Peter Horree/ Alamy, p. 18; prochasson frederic, pp. 18-19; Wikimedia Commons, p. 20; wjarek, p. 21 (Juno); Xirurg, p. 21 (Jupiter); Alexander Demyanenko, p. 21 (Minerva); Marie-Lan Nguyen, p. 21 (Venus); itechno, p. 21 (Mars); Svetlana Pasechnaya, p. 21 (Janus); GL Archive/ Alamy, p. 23 (top); Angelo D'Amico p. 23 (left); RossHelen, p. 23 (middle); Cris Foto, p. 23 (right); Vladimir Korostyshevskiy, p. 25; Waj, p. 26; tichr, pp. 28-29; TTstudio, p. 31.